You have already begun to notice.

This book is where you find your footing.

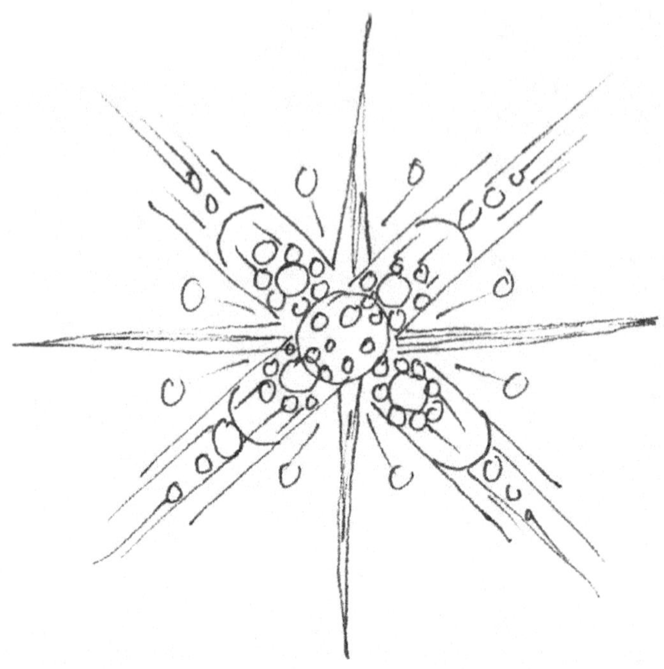

Copyright © 2026 by Swann-Ryder Productions, LLC.

For more information, visit www.ingoswann.com.

First Edition, 2026.
BioMind Superpowers Books.
ISBN-13: 978-1-949214-73-4

You Know More Than You Think
A Five-Book Series

Book Two
Where You Sit
Explorations in Finding Your Footing in a Moving World

Elly Flippen

A BIOMIND SUPERPOWERS BOOK
PUBLISHED BY

Swann-Ryder Productions, LLC

READER GUIDANCE

The following guidance is offered to support safe, grounded, and thoughtful engagement with the practices and explorations presented in this book.

Readers are encouraged to:

> Move at a pace that feels appropriate and sustainable.
> Modify, pause, or discontinue any practice that creates discomfort, distress, or instability.
> Seek qualified professional support when encountering intense emotional, psychological, or perceptual experiences.

The material in this book is not intended to replace sound judgment, professional care, or responsible engagement with daily life, relationships, and decision-making.

These practices are offered as invitations to explore awareness and perceptual literacy, not as doctrines of belief, systems of authority, or substitutes for medical, psychological, or therapeutic care.

Your consent, grounding, safety, and discernment are foundational to your engagement with the material presented here.

TABLE OF CONTENTS

HOW TO APPROACH THIS BOOK

This volume continues the exploration begun in Book One. It is not material to master, but material to move through with attention.

Understanding develops here through direct experience. Some sections may register immediately; others may feel less clear at first. This is natural. Your organismic intelligence differentiates gradually as familiarity deepens.

The pages that follow are designed to guide attention. If something does not resolve right away, allow it to remain open. Recognition often emerges through lived engagement rather than explanation.

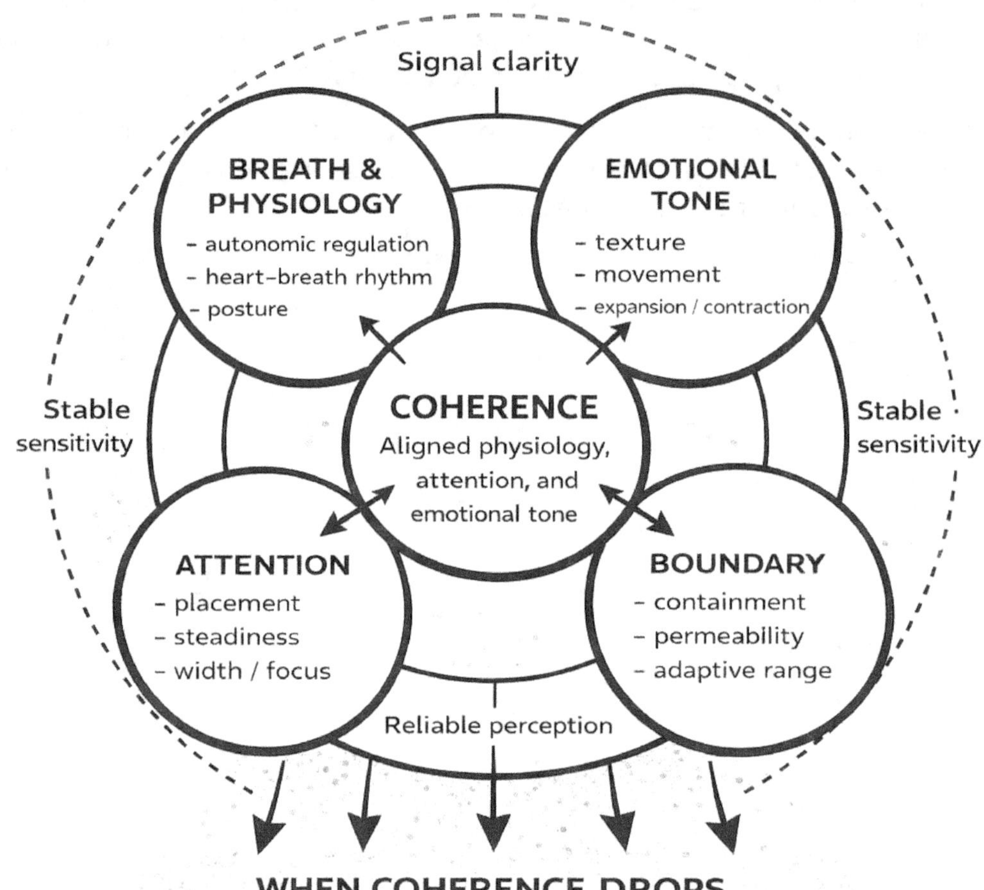

Signal clarity
Stable sensitivity
Stable sensitivity
BREATH & PHYSIOLOGY
- autonomic regulation
- heart-breath rhythm
- posture
EMOTIONAL TONE
- texture
- movement
- expansion / contraction
COHERENCE
Aligned physiology, attention, and emotional tone
ATTENTION
- placement
- steadiness
- width / focus
BOUNDARY
- containment
- permeability
- adaptive range
Reliable perception
WHEN COHERENCE DROPS
- sensory flooding - emotional overwhelm - boundary collapse
- misinterpretation - cognitive interference

The Diagram

The preceding diagram serves as a visual reference for dynamics that become recognizable through experience rather than description. It maps relational processes such as:

> organization and fragmentation
> regulation and overload
> signal and interference
> boundaries as stabilizing functions
> emotion as information

Its relevance may not be immediately apparent. Return to it periodically. As your organismic intelligence differentiates, the diagram will begin to correspond to what you observe in lived experience.

Reading as Experience

This book is meant to be entered, paused within, and revisited directly by you, rather than mediated through instruction or explanation from others.

The chapters build progressively, though not rigidly.

Each introduces distinctions that become clearer through use.

Understanding develops as sensation, emotion, thought, and environmental input become more distinguishable in real time.

Completion is not the objective. Sustained engagement is.

Throughout this book, the word *layer* is used to describe different ways information is organized. In lived experience these are not stacked levels but interdependent functions: simultaneous processes operating together.

The language here is intended to orient attention, not prescribe performance.

The explorations are not tasks to complete correctly, but structured opportunities to observe how your system is already operating.

If something begins to feel effortful, pause. Allow your system to reorganize. Increased differentiation does not arise from force, but from steady engagement.

Nothing new is being installed.

Your organismic intelligence is simply being allowed to function with greater stability, distinction, and reliability.

Pace, Repetition, & Sequence

A useful rhythm may be one chapter per week, allowing time for integration. There is no advantage to speed.

Repetition refines differentiation.

Each return reveals nuance rather than novelty.

What once felt blended begins to separate. What once seemed abstract becomes observable.

The chapters may be read non-sequentially if necessary, though depth increases when the material is encountered in continuity.

Development here is cumulative, though not linear. Recognition often occurs retrospectively.

Trust your timing but remain consistent enough for patterns to emerge.

GETTING READY

Before engaging the explorations, it is useful to establish how to work with them in a way that supports steadiness and continuity within ordinary life.

What follows is not precautionary instruction but an orientation. The aim is stability, not intensity.

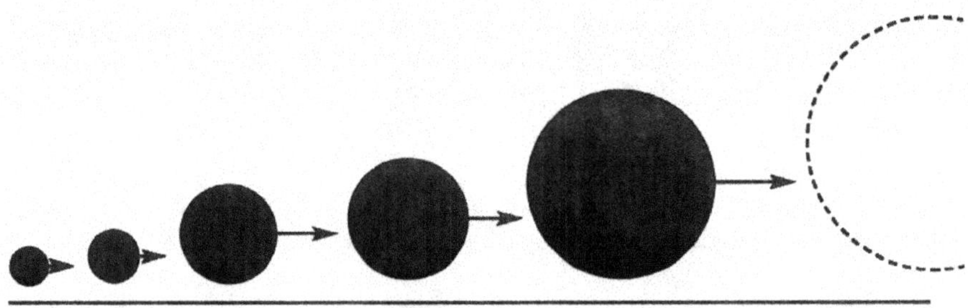
DEVELOPMENT

Approaching the Explorations

This book asks only that you notice your own experience and begin to discern how your system functions.

What you perceive does not become accurate because it feels meaningful, and meaning does not become reliable because it feels vivid.

This material emphasizes direct experience over interpretation. If something does not resonate, there is no need to force it. Organismic perception clarifies through engagement, not agreement.

The explorations that follow are temporary orientations, not states to maintain. They are designed to help you notice specific dynamics. Once an exercise concludes, allow your system to return to its natural baseline.

Each exercise begins and ends. What remains is familiarity, not effort.

Go Slowly

Your system does not reward speed. Reading quickly, stacking practices, or chasing insight often introduces interference rather than clarity.

> Some sections may land gradually and deepen later.
> Some practices may feel subtle rather than dramatic.
> Some understanding may arise days or weeks after reading.

This is not delay. It is integration.

Perception is not an ability one possesses. It is an emergent function of how well the system is organized in the moment. Because that organization is influenced by internal and external conditions, perceptual clarity naturally rises and falls. This fluctuation is not a weakness. It is a signal.

The aim of this work is not permanence, but reliability: supporting the conditions that allow perception to organize itself cleanly.

— Adapted from Ingo Swann, *Psychic Literacy*

Boxed Spaces & Exploration Prompts

Throughout the series, you will find boxed spaces for notes and observations. These are not assignments. They are places for experience to land while it is still forming. Not everything registers as language. Some information appears as:

> sensation
> spatial awareness
> image
> movement
> an unformed impression

Writing or drawing helps stabilize early data without forcing interpretation.

Within each exploration, you will also encounter *What to Watch For* lists and reflection prompts:

> *What to Watch For* lists are orientation points, not guarantees. They highlight common responses so you can recognize shifts rather than overlook them.
> *Reflection* prompts are invitations to engage more directly with your experience. They are not questions to answer correctly. If other questions arise, you are encouraged to follow them as well.

Staying Close to Sensation

Noticing may include images or fleeting impressions. There is no need to interpret them immediately. Early awareness often communicates through sensation and tone before meaning becomes explicit. If something feels charged or unusual, return to the body and remain with what is directly felt.

Meaning develops through familiarity and context, not urgency.

Grounding

If at any point the process feels overwhelming, destabilizing, or "too open," return to what is most basic:

> breath
> posture
> physical sensation
> engagement with the floor or chair
> awareness of the room around you

Clarity begins in the body. It does not replace grounding; it depends on it.

Moments of perceptual intensity or scattered attention simply indicate that your system may need to pause and reorganize.

A One-Minute Reset

1. Pause.
2. Feel a connection with the floor or chair.
3. Let your breath slow naturally.
4. Stay with one sensation in your body.

This is enough. Being aware does not require strain or effort. It begins with simple connection.

Additional reset options are available in the Appendix if you need them

---

Pause If You Need To

If you experience persistent destabilization, intrusive imagery, or difficulty staying oriented in daily life, pause. Return to ordinary routines. Move your body. Rest. Seek support if necessary. Pausing is perceptual maturity.

Key Takeaway

More is always occurring within the body's intelligence than reaches conscious awareness. Perception becomes steadier when you recognize your position within what you are noticing.

When you know where you are situated, perception organizes more clearly. You can remain grounded without being pulled, responsive without being swept away.

Where you stand depends on where you sit.

— Rufus E. Miles Jr.

FINDING YOUR FOOTING IN A MOVING WORLD

SOLID GROUND

By this point, you may have noticed that your awareness extends further than you once assumed. Book Two goes deeper. It does so not by amplifying sensitivity, but by clarifying the structure that organizes it: the underlying architecture that gives perception stability and form.

In this series, sensitivity does not mean fragility, emotional reactivity, or hypersensitivity. It refers to organismic intelligence in motion: the body–attention system registering and noticing information through engagement, proximity, pattern, and change.

Sensitivity is your system's capacity to detect, notice, and make sense of what is present. Whether that sensing becomes coherent or overwhelming depends on how it is organized.

This book invites you to recognize how organismic intelligence is structured and regulated within your body–attention system, and how that organization shapes what you sense, absorb, and respond to, especially in environments of increasing intensity and constant signaling.

Here, you begin to recognize:

> why sensitivity expands and contracts
> why certain interactions feel draining while others feel supportive
> why perception intensifies under stress
> why boundaries soften during emotional load
> how emotional tone shapes what registers
> how repetition and shared attention amplify experience
> how coherence stabilizes perception across the nervous system

If Book One focused on rediscovering your natural sensitivity, Book Two focuses on stabilizing it, so what you perceive remains clear without becoming overwhelming, whether in a crowded room, a charged conversation, or a digital stream of constant input.

This is where familiar experiences begin to make sense:

> walking into a room and immediately sensing its mood
> noticing someone else's tension appear in your own body
> leaving interactions feeling depleted or unsettled
> experiencing "too much" without knowing how to stabilize
> feeling activated by information before you have evaluated it

What often gets labeled as "I just knew" moments (gut recognitions, felt-sense impressions) is not vague or mystical. It is pattern recognition operating below conscious narration.

It reflects prolonged exposure to complex systems: social, emotional, environmental, relational, and informational.

In contemporary terms, this appears as heightened situational awareness, nuanced human judgment, and the ability to detect anomalies before they become explicit.

This is trained organismic intelligence, not something supernatural.

In other words, this book is not about sensing more.

It is about remaining steady while sensing.

You will explore:

> grounding as nervous-system regulation
> relational regulation and boundary maintenance
> perceptual coherence as integrated functioning across body, attention, and emotion
> emotional texture as usable information rather than interference
> presence and proximity (physical or attentional) as relational dynamics that can be noticed without being pulled into reaction

This is also where echoes of Ingo's diagrams begin to appear, not as models to follow, but as early attempts to map territory you are now encountering directly.

His work provides a lineage. Your perception gives it application.

Book Two forms the bridge between:

I notice something happening.

and

I can recognize what I'm sensing and remain grounded while it unfolds.

By the end of this book, sensitivity can become navigable rather than destabilizing, and perceptual coherence becomes something you can return to, not something you lose.

9 I The Coherence Code
Organizing Organismic Perception

Opening Invitation

Coherence arises when the body is sensing, regulating, and orienting in relation to its environment.

You have already encountered it.

You have felt it when:

> your breath steadies
> your posture organizes
> your attention relaxes without strain
> your awareness shifts from scattered to oriented
> sensation becomes clear rather than diffuse

These are not altered states.

They are organized ones.

In Book One, perceptual coherence was introduced as the integrated functioning of sensation, spatial awareness, physiology, and attention.

At that stage, the emphasis was recognition.

Here, we move deeper.

This chapter examines the mechanisms that allow perceptual coherence to form and hold. It explores the regulatory patterns that determine whether the process aligns within itself or competes for dominance.

Coherence is not something added to perception.

It is what perceptual process looks like when its components operate in coordination rather than at cross-purposes.

Organismic perception is always active.

The question is whether it is fragmented or aligned.

This chapter begins to map the organizing principles beneath that alignment: the underlying "code" through which awareness and perception regulate one another, stabilize, and become dependable.

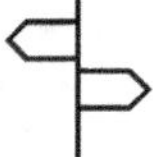

Awareness and perception operate in continuous feedback, an interchange, each updating and reshaping the other.

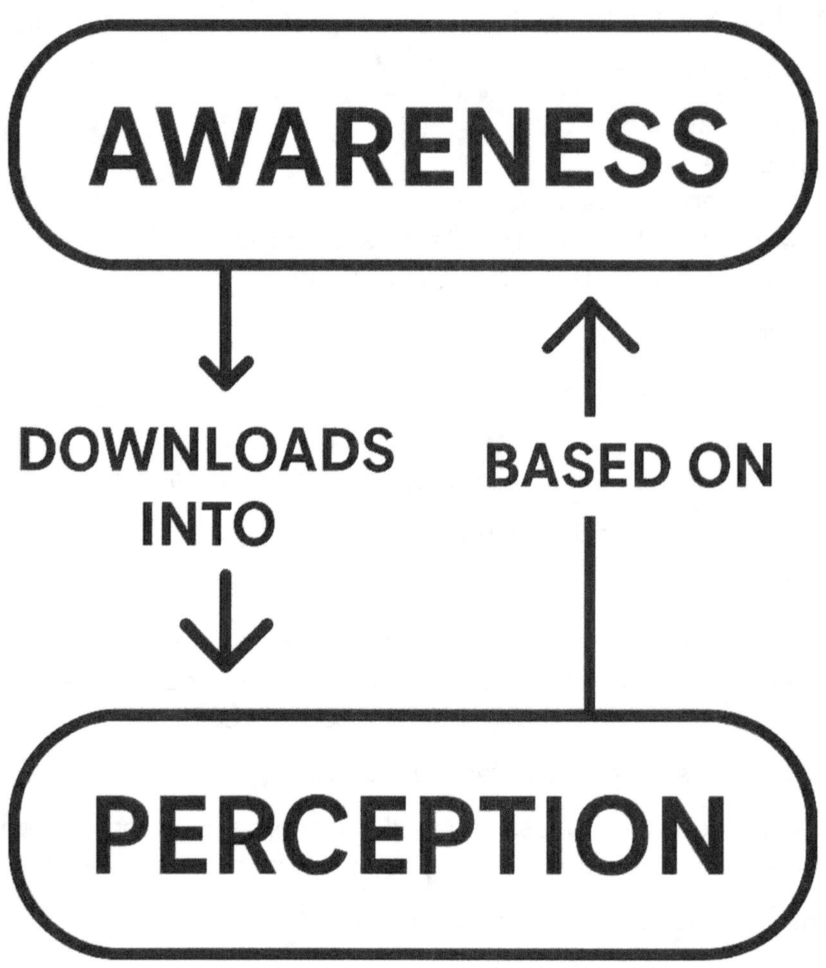

This perceptual-awareness interchange functions as a regulatory loop.

When the loop stabilizes, coherence emerges.

When it destabilizes, fragmentation follows.

Ingo understood perceptual coherence as a form of inner discipline but not discipline in terms of forcing or controlling oneself.

He wrote that "mental self-discipline is the factor that brings one into *phase* (into coherence) with whatever one wishes to take part in and succeed in doing."

When Ingo used the word "phase," he was describing synchronization: a condition in which separate processes operate in rhythm rather than at cross-purposes.

Much like musicians aligning to a shared tempo or people unconsciously matching pace as they walk together, internal systems can come into phase.

In contemporary terms, this refers to coordination among processes such as:

> breath and emotional tone
> attention and intention
> posture and awareness

When these processes align, they support one another rather than interfere. The result is not increased effort, but increased efficiency and reliability.

Seen this way, discipline is not domination; it is organization.

Perceptual coherence is marked by:

> an intellect that is quiet but alert
> sensation that is open yet stable
> breath that is steady
> attention that is grounded and receptive

Sensitivity without stability can become overwhelming. Stability without sensitivity becomes dull. Coherence is where both can coexist.

In this condition, effort softens and the exchange between awareness and perception becomes more reliable.

> Information resolves into recognizable patterns.
> Emotional tone steadies.
> What you perceive becomes usable rather than confusing.

Perceptual coherence emerges from measurable interactions among:

> breath and heart rhythm
> autonomic regulation
> neural coordination
> interoceptive awareness

This chapter offers practical ways to support that organization deliberately.

The aim is not to heighten sensation, but to bring your organismic perception into coherence so sensitivity can deepen without overwhelm and your perception can remain trustworthy without strain.

To organize is to bring parts into a coherent, functioning whole.

— Adapted from Ingo Swann, *Awareness and Perception vs Status of Individual "Realities"*

Notes.

EXPLORATION 9.1: The Heart-Breath Sync
Aligning Emotional & Physiological Rhythm

Objective

To support autonomic coherence by gently synchronizing your breathing rhythm with the natural variability of your heart.

Setup

Sit or stand comfortably with your spine naturally upright. Allow your shoulders to rest easily and your jaw to soften. Your posture should feel supported rather than held rigidly.

Steps

1. Place one hand lightly on the center of your chest to bring your attention toward your heart area.
2. Inhale through your nose for approximately 5 seconds, allowing your breath to move smoothly rather than deeply.
3. Exhale gently through your nose or mouth for approximately 5 seconds.
4. Let your breath feel centered in your chest area rather than forced into your belly or lungs.
5. Continue this rhythm for 1-2 minutes, allowing your body to relax into the pace rather than trying to maintain it perfectly.

What to Watch For

> softening or easing in your chest
> gentle warmth or spreading sensation
> quieting of your mental activity
> increased sense of presence
> what you are aware of expanding without strain

Reflection

↺ Did your emotional tone shift, even slightly?
↺ Did your breathing rhythm feel organizing?
↺ Did your attention become easier to maintain?
↺ Did your body feel more stable or grounded?

Why This Happens

Breathing at a slow, steady rhythm naturally influences your autonomic nervous system, particularly the interaction between breathing and heart rhythm.

The heart generates a strong, rhythmic electrical signal that continuously communicates with the brain through the vagus nerve, blood pressure patterns, and other autonomic pathways. As breath relaxes into a steady pace, this communication begins to coordinate more smoothly.

⟩　During inhalation, heart rate tends to rise slightly.
⟩　During exhalation, heart rate tends to slow.

This natural pattern (known as respiratory sinus arrhythmia) is part of how your body regulates itself continuously. When your breathing rhythm becomes steady, your heart's variability often becomes more coherent as well.

In the language of this book, your system is moving toward coherence.

This synchronization supports perceptual coherence by bringing emotional tone, physiology, and awareness into alignment. It is not simply a relaxation technique, but a coordination process: the physiological basis of centeredness.

Notes.

EXPLORATION 9.2: The Body Alignment Scan
Settling the Body

Objective

To reduce physical interference and support perceptual coherence by allowing your body to organize itself with less effort.

Setup

Sit or stand with your feet grounded and your weight evenly distributed. Allow your body to feel supported rather than held.

Steps

1. Imagine a gentle lift at the crown of your head, as if your spine were lengthening upward without stiffening.
2. Let your shoulders release downward and outward.
3. Soften your jaw, tongue, and muscles around your eyes.
4. Allow your spine to lengthen naturally rather than forcing it straight.
5. Take 1-2 easy breaths while allowing your body to relax into this organization.
6. Slowly scan (place your attention) through your body (from head to feet) and notice any remaining pockets of tension.
7. Where tension is present, allow it to soften slightly without forcing change.

What to Watch For

> Your awareness becoming smoother
> your breath moving more freely
> your mental noise diminishing
> your emotional tone settling toward neutral
> a sense of vertical organization or internal stacking

Reflection

↺ Where did alignment feel interrupted or strained?
↺ Did releasing those areas change how your attention felt?
↺ Did areas of habitual tension seem to affect how your attention felt or organized?

Why Alignment Matters

Postural strain influences several systems at once, including:

> breathing patterns
> muscle tone
> neural signaling
> emotional regulation

When your body is poorly organized, your nervous system must compensate for unnecessary tension and imbalance. Your attention may feel effortful, breathing restricted, and emotional tone more reactive.

When your alignment improves, even slightly, these compensations decrease.

In practical terms, this means that your system no longer must work around physical strain.

Alignment does not create coherence. Rather, it removes obstacles to it and provides the physical scaffold that allows your organismic intelligence to organize and regulate itself naturally.

Notes.

EXPLORATION 9.3: The Mental Reset Switch
Reducing Cognitive Interference

Objective

To briefly interrupt unhelpful mental looping while keeping your intellect available and responsive.

Setup

Anywhere. This reset can be done while sitting, standing, walking, or during conversation. It requires only a brief moment of your attention.

Steps

1. Notice whatever thoughts are currently present without evaluating them or trying to change them.
2. Silently say the word "clear" once, in a neutral tone.
3. Treat the word as a signal rather than a command.
4. Take 1 full, unforced breath.
5. Allow your attention to widen or soften rather than focusing narrowly.
6. Return your attention to physical sensation (such as connection with the floor or chair, the movement of your breath, or the position of your body).

What to Watch For

> your mental activity settling
> increased spaciousness
> emotional signals becoming more recognizable
> your sensitivity sharpening without strain
> reduced internal friction

Reflection

↻ Did what you were aware of feel quieter or more open afterward?
↻ Did what you perceive organize itself differently once thought softened?
↻ Did your attention feel easier to stabilize?

Why This Happens

Signal & Cognitive Noise

Ingo consistently framed perception as a signal-to-noise problem rather than a question of special ability.

Signal refers to meaningful perceptual information already being registered by your system. The raw data.

Noise includes anything that distorts, overwhelms, or obscures that information before it can be recognized.

From this perspective, excessive cognitive activity is not neutral. It functions as noise.

The issue is not thinking itself, but repetitive cognitive looping:

> rumination
> prediction
> internal commentary
> self-monitoring...

...which crowds out signals.

When your intellect cycles through the same material, it introduces competing input into perception.

These signals are louder and faster than subtle sensory information, reducing the signal-to-noise ratio.

The perceptual-awareness interchange process does not usually fail because signal is absent.

It fails because the signal is submerged beneath interference.

The brief reset used in this exploration does not suppress thought. It interrupts habitual looping just long enough for your system to reorganize itself.

When your attention returns to sensation, neural activity shifts from continuous analysis toward integrative sensing. Noise decreases. Signal becomes easier to detect.

A tuned intellect is not an empty one.

It is a less noisy instrument, able to register what was already present.

EXPLORATION 9.4: Whole-System Coherence
Bringing Multiple Systems into Alignment

Objective

To experience perceptual coherence as an emergent state arising from coordinated physiology, attention, and the exchange between perception and awareness.

Setup

Sit or stand comfortably, with minimal external distraction.

Steps

1. Breath.
   - → Inhale for 5 seconds.
   - → Exhale for 5 seconds.
   - → Let the rhythm establish itself.

2. Body.
   - → Adjust your posture until you feel both grounded and gently lifted (stable without tension).

3. Intellect.
   - → Silently say the word "clear" once, neutrally.

4. Heart / Tone.
   - → Allow a mild sense of appreciation, ease, or goodwill to be present, nothing intense, just a steady, positive tone.

5. Awareness.
   - → Let your attention soften and widen rather than drifting outward.
   - → Shift from Spotlight Mode attention (narrow, effortful, target-focused) to Lantern Mode attention (broad, steady, receptive).

6. Hold.
   - → Remain in this organization for 20–30 seconds.
   - → Do not try to intensify the state. Let coordination do the work.

What to Watch For

> warmth or ease in your chest
> subtle tingling or spreading sensation
> alert calm
> emotional neutrality or balance
> your awareness feeling wider but steadier
> a feeling of internal "fit"

Reflection

↺ Did your perceptual coherence feel like something you produced, or something that emerged as systems aligned?

↺ What shifted when your effort dropped?

↺ Did the state feel calm without dullness, alert without strain, and integrated rather than fragmented?

Why This Happens

Perceptual coherence emerges when multiple regulatory systems operate in phase rather than in competition.

Mild positive affect (such as appreciation or ease) has been shown to:

> stabilize heart rhythms
> influence vagal tone
> support attentional regulation
> steady emotional processing

In this context, appreciation is not sentimental.

It functions as a regulatory signal, helping your physiological system and organismic intelligence coordinate.

When your breath, posture, attention, and emotional tone come into alignment, the perceptual-awareness interchange process steadies.

Experience feels integrated rather than divided.

The signal becomes clearer, more reliable, and usable.

Notes.

EXPLORATION 9.5: Perceiving From Coherence
Comparative Perception

Objective

To notice how what you perceive differs when your system is organized into perceptual coherence.

Setup

Choose any exploration from earlier chapters.

Steps

1. Perform the chosen exploration briefly, without preparation.
2. Enter a coherent state using any of the practices from this chapter.
3. Repeat the same exploration.
4. Notice differences in how what you perceive organizes and holds.
5. Do not try to improve the experience. Simply compare.

What to Watch For

> impressions feeling more stable or grounded
> emotional signals becoming comprehensible
> reduced cognitive guessing or commentary
> increased ease or confidence in sensing
> quicker recognition of patterns or relevance
> steadier sense of boundary or orientations

Reflection

↺ What changed when your effort dropped and your organization increased?
↺ Did your system feel more stable, usable, or trustworthy?
↺ What differences did you notice, even if they were subtle?

Notes.

INTEGRATION PRACTICE 9
The 60-Second Coherence Reset

Use anytime.

1. **Breathe:** inhale for 5 seconds, exhale for 5 seconds.
2. **Body:** let your shoulders drop and posture ease.
3. **Intellect:** silently say the word "clear" once.
4. **Tone:** allow a mild sense of appreciation.
5. **Attention:** stabilize what you are aware of in the body.

This takes about 1 minute. Use it before:

> conversations
> relational interactions
> creative work
> difficult or charged moments
> periods of rest or recovery

This sequence does not erase experience. It helps your system adjust so attention, sensation, and emotional tone can operate in alignment. Used regularly, brief resets like this can help support your perceptual-awareness interchange throughout daily life.

Observations.

What must be activated is not something absent, but something obscured.

When the factors that interfere with natural functioning are understood and set aside, the system organizes itself.

— Adapted from Ingo Swann, *Sentiency and Sensitivity*

Notes.

Closing Thought

Perceptual coherence is not advanced.

It is foundational.

When the systems that structure experience detect signals through the body and recognize patterns as a whole, they tend to align rather than compete.

Perceptual information then becomes more reliable and usable.

When perceptual coherence is present:

> information no longer funnels through stress or cognitive overdrive
> meaning organizes without force
> emotional tone steadies
> boundaries strengthen
> orientation becomes evident without strain

This is the engine beneath experience.

> It is accessible, discoverable, and distinctly human.
> It is not something to achieve.

It emerges when interference drops and your organismic intelligence is allowed to function as designed.

10 | The Emotional Frequency Map
Reading Emotional Texture & Tone

Opening Invitation

Emotion is not vague, abstract, or "in your head."

It is a whole-system event: a physiological and perceptual state expressed through texture, temperature, movement, direction, and tone.

We often register emotional information long before we name it. Human beings respond to subtle cues outside conscious detection: changes in posture, tone, rhythm, proximity, and other signals that the body registers before the mind interprets them. In this *sense*, sensing precedes interpretation.

Ingo understood this clearly. He described emotion not as a thought or a story, but as a sensorium condition: a shift within the body–attention system that can be registered before conscious awareness catches up.

Modern science describes these same processes through concepts such as implicit processing, nervous-system regulation, and interoception: the body's capacity to sense its internal state.

Interoception includes breath rhythm, heart variability, muscle tone, visceral sensation, temperature, and internal pressure.

These signals continuously inform the organism about its current condition.

Through interoception, emotional tone is often felt before it is named. What we later describe as a feeling begins as a change in internal organization.

Perceptual researchers have emphasized that emotional states are not merely internal experiences.

They function as organizing influences.

Emotional tone shapes how information is filtered, how proximity is interpreted, and how relational cues are amplified or dampened.

The insight remains consistent: we register far more than we consciously notice.

The deeper question of how meaning forms from these signals will be explored more fully in Book Three.

Here, the emphasis is simpler: discovering how to notice emotional tone as it registers, before interpretation begins.

Before exploring these patterns directly, it helps to visualize the architecture that makes them possible.

The diagram below outlines how what we consciously notice rests upon layered regulatory systems (physiological, relational, and attentional) that continuously organize emotional tone beneath awareness.

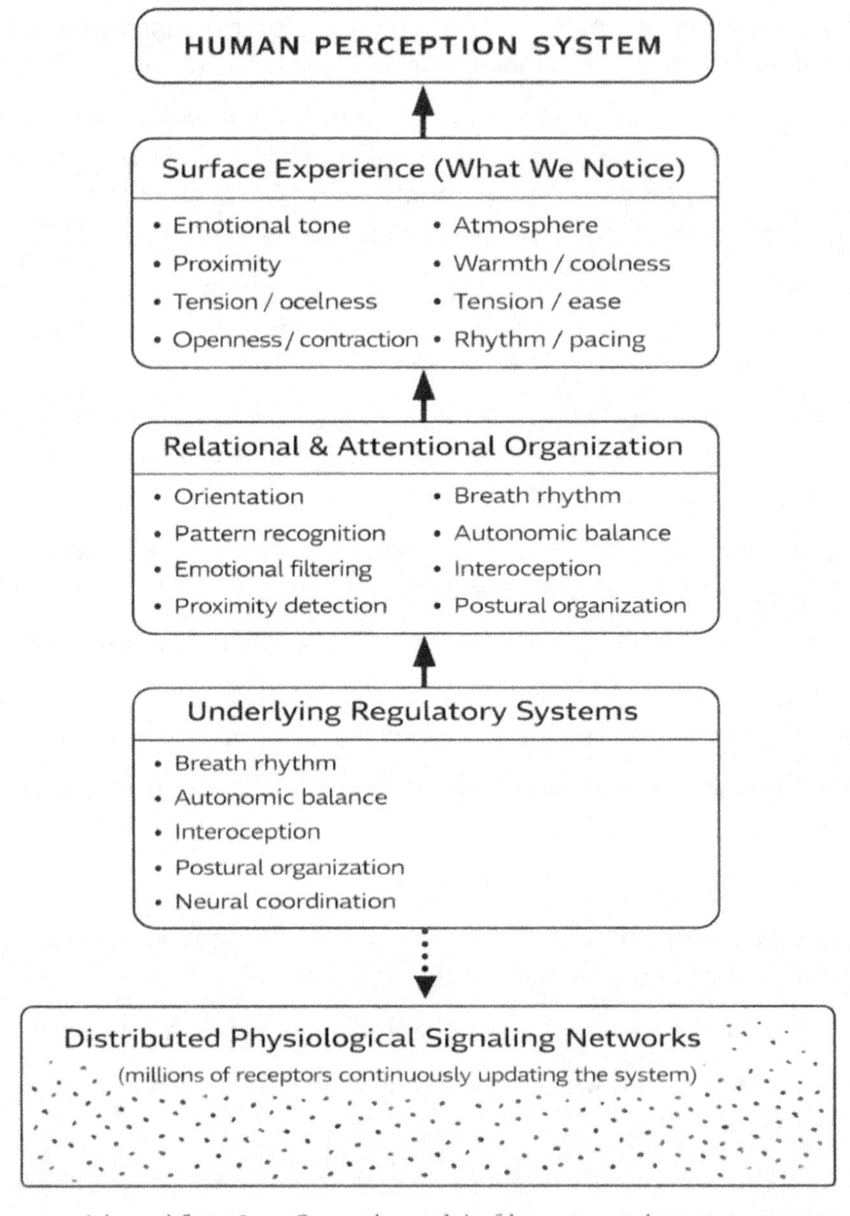

Adapted from Ingo Swann's model of human sensing systems, reframed here in physiological terms.

You may already recognize this:

> a room that feels heavy before anyone speaks
> tension sensed before a facial expression shifts
> warmth or openness around certain people
> a mood that alters an entire space
> the downward pull of grief
> the heat of anger
> the cool openness of calm
> the diffuse warmth of compassion

Emotion is not just a narrative; it is a state the system inhabits.

This chapter explores how emotional tone emerges through the body and attention... and how to recognize those signals without collapsing into them or overanalyzing them.

The aim is not control, suppression, or transcendence, instead it is recognition with stability.

Pause. Check resonance.

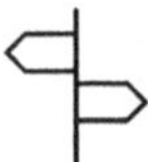

About the Word "Frequency"

In this series, *frequency* is used descriptively, not literally. It refers to how emotional states tend to manifest in experience as:

⟩   movement or stillness
⟩   expansion or contraction
⟩   temperature
⟩   density or lightness
⟩   direction or tone

Throughout the series, tone and frequency are often used interchangeably to describe the felt qualities of emotional states as they register in the body and in perception. The term does not refer to fixed energies, vibrations, or value judgments. No emotional state is better or worse than another. Each carries information.

The Emotional Frequency Map

This map is not a rule. It is a perceptual orientation: a way of recognizing recurring patterns in emotional tone as they register in the body.

The terms that follow (expansive, contracted, neutral, sharp, and soft) are reference points. They describe qualities of tone, movement, and texture, not diagnoses or meanings.

No emotional state fits perfectly into one pattern. Most contain elements of several. The purpose of the map is not to classify experience, but to help you notice how emotion is organizing in the moment before interpretation begins.

Over time, you may refine these distinctions or recognize variations unique to your own system. The map is meant as a starting orientation, something to refine through direct experience. It supports discernment, not diagnosis, and perceptual coherence, not avoidance.

Important Orientation

Emotional tone is information, not instruction.

⟩   **Recognition** does not require agreement.
⟩   **Sensing** does not require action.
⟩   **Stability** allows emotion to be read without being absorbed.

Expansive Patterns

Light, open, or upward movement:

> inspiration
> joy
> appreciation
> spacious love
> curiosity
> openness

Contracted Patterns

Heavy, inward, or downward movement:

> sadness
> fear
> shame
> overwhelm
> depression
> grief

Pause. Check resonance.

Neutral Patterns

Steady, centered, or non-reactive:

> calm
> focus
> contentment
> presence
> composure

Pause. Check resonance.

Sharp Patterns

Hot, pointed, or outward-moving:

> anger
> frustration
> irritation
> aggression

Soft Patterns

Warm, diffuse, surrounding:

> compassion
> empathy
> gentle affection
> acceptance

Pause. Check resonance.

EXPLORATION 10.1: The Internal Scan
Emotional Texture in the Body

Objective

To notice how emotional states take shape through physical sensation and bodily organization.

Setup

Sit comfortably, with minimal external distraction.

Steps

1. Close your eyes or soften your gaze.
2. Ask silently: *What am I feeling right now?*
3. Do not answer with a label, instead, notice sensation directly:
   → Where does it register?
   → Is it still or moving?
   → Does it feel:
      ÷ Heavy or light?
      ÷ Warm or cool?
      ÷ Tight, buzzing, hollow, sharp, soft, diffuse?
4. Only after sensing, choose a word or phrase that seems closest.
5. The word is secondary. The sensation comes first.

What to Watch For

Emotional tone often shows up in patterned ways, though this varies by person:

⟩ chest → connection, sadness, joy, tenderness
⟩ stomach / gut → fear, anticipation, unease
⟩ throat → expression, restraint, readiness
⟩ head → pressure, activation, overwhelm
⟩ whole body → expansion, contraction, settling

Reflection

↺ Did the emotion have a discernible temperature, movement, or density?
↺ How did sensing first change the way you named it?

Why Emotions Have Location

Emotional states involve coordinated activity across the nervous system, muscles, hormones, and autonomic regulation.

Different emotions recruit different patterns of activation, which is why they tend to be felt in distinct areas of the body.

Emotion is not abstract. It is embodied organization.

Navigating through how to notice where and how emotion shows up in your body allows you to recognize it without collapsing into it or explaining it away.

Notes.

EXPLORATION 10.2: Object Resonance
Emotional Association Through Physical Items

Objective

To observe how emotional memory and association emerge somatically through contact with objects.

Setup

Find two objects (choose objects that feel appropriate to handle calmly):

1. One associated with positive, supportive, or neutral experience.
2. One associated with stress, difficulty, or unresolved experience.

Steps

1. Hold the first object in your hands.
2. Stay with the sensation for several breaths.
3. Notice any internal shifts without analysis.
4. Set it down.
5. Hold the second object and repeat.
6. Compare how your system responds.
7. Do not try to recall stories. Let sensation lead.

What to Watch For

⟩ warmth versus coolness
⟩ openness versus tightening
⟩ smoothness versus density
⟩ uplift versus heaviness
⟩ expansion versus contraction

Reflection

↺ How did your body respond differently to each object?
↺ Was the contrast obvious, understated, or mixed?

Why This Happens

Objects do not carry emotion as an external property. You carry the association.

When you touch an object, sensory input activates memory, context, and expectation simultaneously. These associations are expressed through changes in posture, breath, muscle tone, and emotional state, often before conscious recall.

This exploration builds emotional literacy by helping you distinguish:

> what is present now
> from what is being recalled
> from how your body responds automatically

The object does not create the response. It reveals it.

Notes.

EXPLORATION 10.3: The Distance Effect
Emotional Tone Without Proximity or Conversation

Objective

To notice how emotional tone becomes apparent at a distance through your own bodily responses, without interaction, interpretation, or inference.

Setup

Choose someone to observe briefly and respectfully, either in a public setting or with a willing, trusted partner. (This is quiet noticing, not analysis.)

Steps

1. Soften your gaze into a relaxed, unfocused attention.
2. Let your attention rest lightly in the person's general direction.
3. Without naming emotions, notice broad qualities:
    → heavy / light
    → warm / cool
    → sharp / soft
    → contracted / expanded
4. Shift your attention to your own body and notice micro-responses:
    → subtle tightening or softening in your chest or belly
    → your breath changing slightly
    → a faint lean-in or lean-away
    → warmth or coolness in your hands
    → tension or release in your jaw or throat
5. Withdraw your attention completely.
6. Compare your internal state before, during, and after. Remain neutral. Do not try to explain what you notice.

What to Watch For

> changes in your internal "temperature" or density
> ease versus hesitation
> your breath responding without intention
> small postural adjustments
> shifts that disappear when your attention withdraws

Reflection

- ↻ Which part of your body responded first? (Chest, belly, breath, posture, jaw, hands, etc.)
- ↻ Did the response feel immediate or gradual?
- ↻ Did the sensation feel informational or emotional?
- ↻ What changed when you withdrew attention?
- ↻ Did the response fade, settle, or linger after withdrawal?
- ↻ Was the information more apparent when you stayed neutral rather than curious or evaluative?

Why This Happens

Before your intellect engages, your organismic intelligence continuously evaluates relational cues through posture, breath, muscle tone, facial expression, timing, and autonomic shifts.

These responses occur faster than conscious interpretation.

What you are noticing is not the other person's inner state directly, but your own system's response to subtle signals: patterns of movement, orientation, rhythm, pressure, behavioral pacing, and emotional tone expressed through the body.

This is the physiological basis of what people casually call "vibes" or "chemistry."

These are not invisible forces within a mystical framework, but complex constellations of physical and behavioral information sensed in their raw form before they are labeled.

Ingo described such impressions as being registered directly through the sensorium as bodily shifts in tension, warmth, contraction, expansion, or alertness rather than as ideas.

What feels intangible is often simply rapid, pre-verbal pattern recognition.

When two systems begin responding to one another in this way, a natural form of rapport can emerge: a relationship marked by harmony, alignment, or mutual responsiveness. Breath rhythm may synchronize, pacing may match, and emotional tone may begin to stabilize between people.

In this condition perception becomes sympathetic in the original sense of the word, not sentimental, but responsive through affinity and mutual sensitivity.

Your organismic intelligence begins registering shifts in the emotional tone of others and adjusting accordingly.

The contrast between engagement and withdrawal helps distinguish:

> perception from projection
> sensing from assumption
> signal from imagination

This exploration helps build discernment by keeping your attention anchored in sensation rather than conclusion.

Notes.

We become shaped by what we are able to sense and feel.

What does not reach our own system remains, for us, largely unreal.

When sensitivity expands, so does connection with what others are carrying.

Awareness of relational tone, strain, imbalance, or distress becomes more immediate.

This does not grant special powers; it increases exposure instead.

With increased sensitivity comes increased responsibility: the capacity to recognize disharmony, suffering, or instability as lived conditions rather than abstract ideas.

— Adapted from Ingo Swann, *The Topic of the Human Species Guild Revisited Six Years Later*

Notes.

EXPLORATION 10.4: The Frequency Shift
Changing Emotional Tone Deliberately

Note

This exercise is about modulation, not avoidance. The goal is not to bypass emotion, but to experience how emotional tone can change when conditions change.

When Not to Shift

Not every emotional state should be adjusted immediately.

There are times when emotion is signaling something that requires attention rather than alteration. In these moments, changing tone too quickly can obscure important information.

Do not use this practice to override emotion when:

> you are receiving a clear signal about safety, boundaries, or harm
> grief or loss needs space to be acknowledged
> anger is pointing to a violated value or unmet need
> fear is providing orientation rather than dysregulation
> emotional intensity is part of natural processing

Emotions often stabilize on their own when they are allowed to fully take shape and be felt without judgment.

Modulation becomes appropriate after:

> the signal has been recognized
> the emotional state has been acknowledged
> the information has been received

This exploration is about discernment, not control.

The aim is not emotional neutrality, but emotional responsiveness.

Perceptual coherence includes the capacity to remain with what is present before choosing how to respond.

Objective

To experience emotions as dynamic, responsive states rather than fixed identities.

Setup

Sit or stand comfortably, with minimal distraction.

Steps

1. Identify your current emotional tone using sensation rather than labels.
2. Choose a tone you would prefer to inhabit:
    → calm
    → curiosity
    → appreciation
    → steady presence
3. Bring to mind an anchor that naturally evokes that tone:
    → a memory
    → a physical sensation
    → a familiar environment
4. Let your breath support the shift without forcing it.
5. Notice what changes first.
6. Stay until the new tone feels stable or firmly established.

What to Watch For

⟩ your chest softening or expansion
⟩ release of tension
⟩ your breath slowing or deepening
⟩ your attention widening
⟩ reduction in your mental noise

Reflection

↺ Could you notice the shift before you named it?
↺ What changed first: breath, posture, sensation, or attention?
↺ Did the new tone feel imposed or emergent?
↺ Did the original emotion dissolve, soften, or reorganize?
↺ How stable did the new tone feel over time?

Why This Happens

Emotional frequency is not fixed.

It reflects ongoing interaction among multiple regulatory processes:

> autonomic balance
> breath rhythm
> muscle tone and posture
> attentional weighting
> memory and contextual interpretation

These processes are continuously updating one another. Emotional tone is the felt expression of their coordination.

When one or more of these conditions shifts, the overall pattern shifts with it.

> A slower exhale alters autonomic bias.
> A change in posture affects muscle tone and breathing.
> A widening of attention reduces the amplification of a single signal.

This is not suppression.

Suppression attempts to override emotion through force or denial.

Regulation works differently. It alters the conditions that sustain a pattern.

By shifting attention and physiological context, you reduce the dominance of one emotional configuration and create space for a broader, more coherent state to emerge.

The original emotion is not erased.

It is rebalanced within a larger system of regulation and awareness.

This is systematic regulation: emotion responding to changed conditions rather than being overridden by effort.

In this way, modulation becomes an act of alignment, not control.

Notes.

EXPLORATION 10.5: The Two-Person Frequency Dance
Perceiving Emotional Interaction

Objective

To observe how two emotional states interact through blending, amplification, softening, or repulsion without interpretation or analysis.

Setup

Work with a trusted partner. Choose a clam, neutral environment.

Steps

1. Sit or stand facing each other, approximately 3–5 feet apart.
2. Each person silently chooses an emotional tone to hold (not perform).
3. Close your eyes or soften your gaze.
4. Bring your attention to the space between you rather than focusing on your partner directly.
5. Notice:
   → Does one tone feel more dominant?
   → Do the tones blend or remain distinct?
   → Is there a push, pull, or neutrality?
   → Does the atmosphere feel denser, lighter, warmer, cooler, sharper, or softer?
6. Afterward, share which emotional tone each of you chose.

What to Watch For

⟩ interference or distortion or amplification
⟩ softening or neutralization / merging or overlap
⟩ push or pull (warmth, pressure, or spatial change)

Reflection

↺ Did the emotional interaction register more as texture, direction, temperature, or movement?
↺ Did your own body change as the shared tone formed?
↺ Was the interaction stable, shifting, or asymmetrical?
↺ Did naming the emotions afterward confirm, clarify, or complicate what you sensed?

Why This Happens

When two emotional systems come into proximity, they interact through physiology rather than intention. Bodily systems co-regulate via posture, breath, muscle tone, facial micro-expression, and attentional orientation.

These interactions can:

> amplify or intensify
> soften or stabilize
> interfere or cancel
> harmonize or compete

This is not symbolic or metaphorical. It is relational physiology in action.

What people describe as chemistry, comfort, tension, or conflict begins here: emotional frequency interacting before words or meaning intervene.

You are not reading emotion as an idea. You are noticing how emotional states behave when they meet.

Notes.

INTEGRATION PRACTICE 10
The Daily Frequency Check

Several times a day, ask:

1. What is my emotional tone right now? (No analysis, just notice.)
2. Where do I sense it in my body? (Location, temperature, density, movement.)
3. How is it shaping perception? For example:
    → heavy → narrower focus
    → calm → wider awareness
    → fear → contraction
    → curiosity → expansion
4. Can this frequency shift slightly if conditions change? (Through breath, posture, attention, or grounding.)
5. What changes in interaction when my tone shifts? (Notice responses in others, space, or atmosphere. This reflects how emotional tone radiates into the environment.)

This practice is not about correcting emotion. It is about tracking influence: how emotional tone organizes perception, attention, and relationship constantly. Over time, this builds emotional literacy without suppression and regulation without force.

Observations.

Closing Thought

Emotions are not obstacles to perception.

They are perception, one of the primary ways your system orients to the world.

Every emotion carries a felt pattern: shape, tone, movement, and direction.

When emotion is sensed as experience rather than story:

> clarity increases
> reactivity softens
> boundaries strengthen
> awareness steadies
> connection becomes deliberate
> sensitivity becomes resilience

You are not at the mercy of emotional weather.

You are learning to read it, and, when appropriate, to gently influence the conditions that shape it.

As emotional frequency becomes easier to recognize, interaction itself begins to change.

Perception becomes more responsive, less reactive. Alignment replaces resistance, and connection becomes more deliberate.

Organismic intelligence does not require emotional absence.

It requires emotional literacy: the ability to read emotional tone.

11 | Boundaries
What a Boundary Is

Opening Invitation

In Book One, you explored personal space directly: noticing how proximity, orientation, and approach altered sensation. You observed where contact felt comfortable and where alertness increased. Here, we go deeper.

Boundaries are not lines you draw; they are conditions your system maintains.

Each person has a natural perimeter: a distance, density, and quality of connection that regulates interaction.

This perimeter is not fixed. It adjusts continuously in response to safety, context, and your internal state. When that perimeter is crossed without consent, your body responds immediately:

> a tightening in the chest
> a pull in the belly
> a shift in breath
> an urge to step back
> heightened alertness

These responses are not ideas. They are regulatory events.

In Book One, you noticed the felt edge of your space. In this chapter, you begin to understand the architecture that maintains it.

Boundaries are not merely psychological constructs. They are biological processes expressed through personal space, autonomic adjustment, and interoceptive signaling.

The limits of a living system are not only anatomical or conceptual, but perceptual; a reality Ingo recognized early in his work. A boundary is not where awareness begins. It is where responsiveness increases. It marks the threshold at which monitoring becomes engagement.

A boundary is not a wall. It is an adaptive interface: biological, perceptual, and relational. Your boundary continuously reorganizes:

> expanding in conditions of safety
> contracting under stress
> sharpening when vigilance increases

It is not imagined. It is regulated.

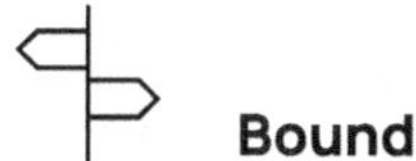

Boundaries

What a Boundary Actually Is

Boundaries are often described as rules, preferences, or interpersonal agreements. This is useful, but incomplete.

A lived boundary is:

> the edge of your perceptual space
> the distance at which your nervous system feels safe
> the point where external signals shift from neutral to intrusive
> the subtle line where your system records yes or no
> a dynamic, responsive membrane

Boundaries shift with:

> emotional state
> environment
> relational context
> regulatory capacity
> attention
> coherence

The Two Forms of Boundaries

1. **Physical Boundary:** Your skin and the immediate space around the body.
2. **Perceptual Boundary:** The felt perimeter where your system begins responding to contact. This may be physical proximity, relational intensity, focused attention, or repeated signaling. Often within a few feet. Sometimes across a room. Sometimes across a screen.

You already know this boundary through experience:

> someone steps too close → you pull back
> someone stands behind you → your shoulders tense
> someone you trust → their presence softens
> someone overwhelming → your system contracts
> repeated or emotionally charged content → your breath shifts or tone tightens

This is not overreaction. This is regulation.

The Five Boundary States

Boundaries are not static. They shift with nervous system regulation, emotional load, environment, and relationship.

These shifts tend to organize into five recognizable states.

1. **Open:** Physiology: parasympathetic tone increases.

> → perceptual space feels wide and receptive
> → signals register as safe rather than invasive
> → common during creativity, trust, intimacy, and time in nature

2. **Neutral:** Physiology: balanced autonomic state; alert but relaxed.

> → clear, present, grounded
> → neither guarded nor porous
> → ideal for everyday functioning and decision-making

3. **Contracted:** Physiology: sympathetic activation rises; posture narrows.

> → perceptual space pulls inward
> → vigilance increases
> → boundaries tighten to reduce stimulation

4. **Spiked:** Physiology: fight-or-flight activation.

> → boundary feels sharp or reactive
> → defensive edge
> → common under threat, pressure, or intrusion

5. **Dissolved:** Physiology: shutdown or freeze responses; numbness; depletion.

> → boundary becomes unclear or collapsed
> → difficulty distinguishing self from other
> → common in fatigue, trauma responses, or chronic people-pleasing

Recognizing these states is not about judgment.

It is about real-time self-awareness.

Your boundary communicates capacity and comfort before your intellect explains it.

61

Healthy Boundaries Aren't Hard. They're Clear

Many people imagine boundaries as rigid walls.

In perceptual terms, a boundary is not hardness, rather it is clarity.

A clear boundary differentiates without hardening.

A healthy boundary allows you to:

⟩ stay present without becoming overwhelmed
⟩ connect without merging
⟩ sense others without absorbing them
⟩ remain open without collapsing

Strong boundaries tend to feel like:

⟩ groundedness
⟩ calm
⟩ confidence
⟩ emotional privacy
⟩ steady presence

Weak or unclear boundaries often appear as:

⟩ confusion
⟩ emotional merging
⟩ anxiety
⟩ exhaustion
⟩ porousness
⟩ absorbing moods or tension

Healthy boundaries do not force a choice between openness and protection.

They allow both, in proportion to context and capacity.

The purpose of this chapter is not to build walls.

It is to help you notice your boundary as a living membrane (one that can expand, contract, or stabilize) so you can move among people and environments with clarity rather than confusion.

EXPLORATION 11.1: Boundary Modulation Scan
Tracking the Expansion & Contraction of Your Boundary

Objective

To observe how your perceptual boundary expands, contracts, and stabilizes in response to internal regulation.

Setup

Stand comfortably with both of your feet grounded and your posture relaxed.

Steps

1. Close your eyes or soften your gaze.
2. Focus on your body as it is, without changing anything.
3. Let your attention extend outward in all directions.
4. Gradually widen that attention, about 12 inches, then 2 feet, then 3 feet or more.
5. Notice where a shift occurs, such as:
   → subtle resistance
   → a change in pressure
   → a felt "stop" or "wait"
   → thinning or fading of sensation
   → a sense of open or neutral space beyond
6. Do not force expansion. Let the boundary reveal itself.
7. Take 1 slow breath and soften your body.
8. Notice whether your perimeter shifts.
9. Now recall a mildly stressful memory.
10. Notice whether your perimeter changes again.

What to Watch For

⟩ a ring or band of subtle sensation
⟩ tingling or activation near the perimeter
⟩ gentle inward or outward pressure
⟩ a neutral, quiet edge rather than a sharp line

Reflection

↺ Did your boundary shift with breath?

↻ Did it change with emotional recall?
↻ Was your boundary consistent or adaptive?
↻ Did it feel permeable, firm, diffuse, or variable?

Why This Happens

Your system does not maintain a fixed perimeter. It continuously adjusts the range at which it monitors, engages, or protects.

As such, your boundary is not fixed structure. It is adaptive architecture.

This adjustment is shaped by:

> autonomic regulation
> emotional load
> fatigue or coherence
> perceived safety
> context

The boundary you detect is a regulatory threshold: the point at which your system shifts from neutral awareness to increased readiness.

When you soften your breath, your boundary may expand. When you recall stress, it may contract. By observing these shifts directly, you are noticing how your system organizes proximity in real time.

In Book One, you located your boundary's edge. Here, you observe its flexibility.

Notes.

Because human beings are continuously influenced by social processes, the boundary between personal signals and relational influence is often subtle and difficult to detect.

— Adapted from Ingo Swann, *Contaminants and "Noise"*

Notes.

EXPLORATION 11.2: Relational Boundary
Where Self & Other Begin to Meet

Objective

To observe how your boundary reorganizes in response to relational cues.

Setup

Work with a trusted partner in a still, open, quiet space.

Steps

1. Stand comfortably, facing away from your partner.
2. Your partner begins 10–15 feet behind you.
3. Ask your partner to walk slowly and steadily toward you.
4. Pay attention to any internal signal that indicates a shift in your boundary (tension, alertness, emotional change, or a sense of "someone entering your space").
5. Say "stop" the moment you notice an evident internal response.
6. Turn and observe the distance between you.

Variations
(Repeat the same exercise while changing one condition at a time.)

Approach direction, your partner approaches from:

1. The front.
2. The side.
3. A diagonal angle.

Relational cues, repeat the approach after:

1. Briefly making eye contact.
2. A friendly verbal cue.
3. While your partner intentionally stiffens their posture.

What to Watch For

> rising alertness, increased vigilance, or ease
> warmth, tingling, or pressure
> changes in your breath or posture
> a shift in your emotional tone

Reflection

- ↺ Did familiarity alter the distance?
- ↺ Did tone or posture change your perimeter?
- ↺ Did your boundary feel protective, receptive, or neutral?
- ↺ Did regulation in your partner influence your own response?
- ↺ Did your internal boundary shift depending on variation cues?

Why This Happens

The nervous system continuously detects changes in proximity and interprets them in milliseconds.

But boundary response is not driven by distance alone. It is shaped by multiple relational signals, including:

- ⟩ relational tone
- ⟩ posture and coherence in the other person
- ⟩ familiarity and trust
- ⟩ your own regulatory state

A calm, regulated presence may allow your boundary to expand.

An abrupt or tense approach may cause it to contract.

What you are observing is not simply the detection of proximity.

You are observing co-regulation.

Your boundary functions as a relational interface. It mediates exchange before contact, before speech, before conscious decision.

In Book One, you noticed that approach is detectable. Here, you observe how your boundary reorganizes in response to context and relationship.

This reveals that your boundary is not merely a defense, but a form of adaptive coordination.

EXPLORATION 11.3: The Compression Effect

The Elasticity of Your Boundary

Objective

To experience your boundary as responsive and adjustable rather than fixed.

Setup

Stand comfortably with your feet grounded and your posture relaxed.

Steps

1. On an inhale, allow your sense of space to gently expand outward, approximately 2–4 feet.
2. On an exhale, let that sense of space draw in closer, about 6–12 inches around your body.
3. Repeat this cycle several times without forcing either movement.
4. Notice how your emotional tone, posture, and internal state shift with each cycle.

What to Watch For

> expansion → openness, warmth, spaciousness
> contraction → containment, strength, protection
> a natural preference emerging in this moment

Reflection

↺ Which state felt more supportive right now: expansion or contraction?
↺ What shifted when you realized you could influence the size and tone of your boundary?
↺ Did either state feel stabilizing rather than limiting?

Why This Happens

Your perceptual boundary naturally expands and contracts with autonomic state. When your breath is paired intentionally with expansion or contraction:

> inhalation supports openness and outward orientation
> exhalation supports containment and inward regulation

This exploration demonstrates that boundaries are not passive reactions imposed by others.

They are adaptive states, influenced by breath, attention, and nervous-system regulation.

Experiencing this flexibility directly restores agency and gives less weight to the idea that boundaries must be either too rigid or too porous. A boundary can be firm without being closed, and open without being unprotected.

Notes.

EXPLORATION 11.4: Somatic "No" & "Yes"
Somatic Consent

Objective

To notice early bodily signals of alignment or resistance before your intellect takes over.

Setup

Sit or stand comfortably in a neutral environment. Choose a moment when you are not rushed, pressured, or emotionally charged.

This exploration works best with ordinary, low-stakes choices rather than highly emotional decisions.

Steps

1. Bring to mind an action, invitation, or choice you are considering.
2. Before thinking it through, notice whether your body registers:
   → openness
   → lift or subtle forward movement
   → warmth or expansion
3. Now bring to mind something you definitely do not want.
4. Notice whether your body registers:
   → contraction
   → tightening or backward movement
   → heaviness, density, or closing
5. Do not judge or analyze the response. Let it appear.

What to Watch For

〉 forward / open vs. backward / closed orientation
〉 chest or belly shifts: expansion vs. tightening
〉 smooth vs. dense internal quality
〉 immediacy of response (signals arising before thought)
〉 consistency of sensation across repetitions

Reflection

- ↻ Did the response arise before reasoning or explanation?
- ↻ Which sensations felt most stable or repeatable?
- ↻ Did "yes" feel grounded rather than urgent?
- ↻ Did "no" feel protective rather than reactive?

Why This Happens

Your nervous system continuously evaluates safety, fit, and alignment. These evaluations register somatically through posture, muscle tone, breath, and visceral sensation before they reach conscious thought.

This exploration does not ask you to decide or act. It simply brings pre-conscious signals into active awareness without forcing interpretation.

You are not choosing here. You are navigating through how to recognize how your system communicates before your intellect takes over.

Notes.

High-Intensity Presence & Boundary Load

Not all boundary challenges arise from intrusion or threat. Some arise from amplification.

Highly energized people and environments (charismatic leaders, performers, crowds, rallies, concerts, or moments of collective excitement) can place unusual load on perceptual boundaries, even when nothing unsafe is occurring.

In these contexts, your system is not responding to danger. It is responding to amplified signaling.

Your nervous system is designed to orient toward heightened activation. → Heightened activation suggests relevance. → Relevance draws attention.

When many individuals orient toward the same stimulus, posture, breath, vocal tone, and emotional rhythm begin to synchronize.

Activation organizes collectively rather than individually.

The result can be a shared surge of arousal that feels uplifting, overwhelming, intoxicating, or destabilizing, depending on boundary clarity and regulation.

You may recognize this when:

⟩ a crowd's excitement moves through you before you consciously decide how you feel
⟩ someone's charisma draws your attention strongly toward them
⟩ emotion escalates rapidly in a group without deliberate coordination
⟩ your own state shifts dramatically in the presence of a performer or leader
⟩ you feel energized during the event, then depleted afterward

This is not imagination. It is not weakness.

It is boundary permeability under high stimulation.

In high-activation environments, boundaries often:

⟩ expand quickly
⟩ soften or thin
⟩ synchronize with collective rhythm
⟩ narrow focus toward the shared stimulus
⟩ blur differentiation between self and group

When this occurs, emotional tone and arousal spread rapidly. Excitement amplifies excitement. Anxiety amplifies anxiety. Attention locks in. Individual regulation may temporarily yield to collective momentum.

Meaning may follow activation rather than precede it.

This helps explain how:

> emotional waves move through crowds
> people feel bonded without personal intimacy
> activation escalates faster than interpretation
> clarity decreases even as energy rises

The experience can be powerful. It can also be disorienting.

A defined boundary does not block these experiences.

It regulates how much of them you absorb.

With boundary clarity:

> you can feel activation without losing orientation
> excitement arises without hijacking decision-making
> admiration does not collapse into merging
> inspiration does not override discernment
> participation does not require surrender

Without boundary clarity, your system may spike, dissolve, or shut down afterward, often experienced as exhaustion, confusion, or "I don't know what happened."

Boundaries allow vitality without consumption, and intensity without capture.

Pause. Check resonance.

EXPLORATION 11.5: The Crowd Regulation Check
Staying Oriented in High-Activation Environments

Safety Orientation: High-Intensity Group Settings

Group settings amplify attention and emotion. Amplification increases boundary load and may cause perceptual space to widen, emotional tone to synchronize, and grounding to thin.

The aim is not to block experience; it is to remain oriented while participating.

If clarity drops or you feel swept up, return your attention to your body: feel your feet, slow your breath, reestablish your boundary.

Pausing or stepping back is regulation, not withdrawal.

Objective

To experience how your boundary responds to collective activation and to practice staying grounded without disconnecting.

Setup

Use this exploration in a real-world setting: a concert, lecture, performance, rally, conference, or crowded public space. You may also practice briefly while watching a performance or speech on a screen.

Steps

1. Begin by establishing a connection to the environment through your feet or seat. Let your posture organize naturally.
2. Notice your breath without altering it.
3. Let your attention rest on the collective activation pattern: sound, movement, emotional tone, shared focus.
4. Without analysis, notice:
   - → Is your boundary expanding, thinning, or tightening?
   - → Is your emotional tone shifting rapidly or steadily?
5. On an exhale, gently firm your boundary just enough to restore differentiation (not to shut down).
6. Continue engaging with the environment while maintaining that containment.

Disengage

7. When ready to exit (or briefly pause), deliberately withdraw your attention inward.
8. Feel your feet or seat again.
9. Lengthen 1 exhale.
10. Let your boundary return to its natural resting width.
11. Notice what emotional tone remains once collective activation is no longer amplified.

What to Watch For

> sudden surges of excitement or emotion
> your attention pulled outward without deliberate choice
> loss of internal reference points
> relief when containment returns
> clarity increasing without loss of engagement

Reflection

↺ Did clarity increase when you stabilized your boundary?
↺ Could you participate without absorbing the full activation?
↺ Did containment feel grounding rather than restrictive?

Why This Happens

In group environments, attention naturally synchronizes. Shared rhythm, sound, and focus align posture, breath, and emotional tone across individuals.

Without boundary awareness, this synchronization can temporarily override individual regulation. Your system can shift from self-referenced to group-referenced.

By maintaining a defined boundary while staying present, you interrupt automatic merging. You allow collective activation to be present without allowing it to dictate your internal organization.

This preserves discernment.

> It reduces post-event depletion.
> It keeps perception coherent rather than intoxicating.

Notes.

The Invisible Crowd

What once entered through a single screen at predictable hours now follows you in your pocket.

The attention environment no longer waits for you to sit before it.

It orients toward you, adapts to your patterns, and reflects them back amplified.

Digital environments generate activation without physical proximity.

You may feel aligned, outraged, inspired, or bonded without ever entering a shared room. The system does not require bodies in space to synchronize. It responds to signaling.

Repetition increases salience. → Salience draws attention. → Attention elevates arousal. → Elevated arousal narrows perception.

When emotionally charged material repeats, your body begins to coordinate with it. Your breath shifts. Your muscle tone adjusts. Your emotional tone rises or contracts. Identity language strengthens. Your system organizes around what it encounters most frequently.

This is not dramatic manipulation. It is exposure shaping regulation.

In physical crowds, synchrony emerges through shared rhythm, sound, posture, and proximity. In digital environments, synchrony emerges through repetition, visibility, and collective reaction. The cues differ. The regulatory effect is similar.

Emotional tone spreads rapidly when:

⟩ content is repeated
⟩ language becomes urgent
⟩ threat or triumph is implied
⟩ belonging is signaled
⟩ opposition is emphasized

Under these conditions, boundaries may:

⟩ widen without awareness
⟩ thin through constant exposure
⟩ synchronize with collective tone
⟩ lose fine differentiation
⟩ substitute reaction for reflection

You may recognize this when:

> your emotional state shifts before evaluation
> you feel bonded to people you have never met
> outrage feels clarifying rather than activating
> repetition increases certainty
> stepping away feels uncomfortable or disorienting

This is boundary permeability under amplified signaling.

Your system is designed to orient toward heightened activation. Heightened activation suggests relevance. Relevance draws attention. Repeated attention narrows perception.

When perceptual coherence drops:

> urgency replaces curiosity
> emotional tone intensifies
> identity language strengthens
> nuance diminishes
> withdrawal feels like loss

Your system organizes around the dominant signal.

Over time, borrowed emotion can begin to feel personal. Collective tone can feel like individual conviction. Reaction can resemble discernment.

None of this requires ill intent. It reflects how regulation responds to sustained input.

Boundary clarity allows activation to be evaluated rather than automatically internalized.

With boundary clarity:

> you can engage without merging
> activation can be felt without becoming identity
> repetition does not automatically become truth
> emotional tone can be noticed without being carried forward
> stepping away restores rather than destabilizes

You remain oriented.

One way to assess boundary clarity in digital environments is simple:

1. Withdraw attention briefly.
2. Set the device down.
3. Let your breath lengthen.

4. Allow your posture to reorganize.
5. Notice whether your emotional tone persists or settles.

Signal that remains stable under perceptual coherence deserves examination.

Signal that intensifies under repetition but softens under regulation is likely amplified arousal rather than grounded perception.

This is not a call to avoid activation. It is an invitation to notice how it organizes you.

Activation is not the problem.

Perimeter collapse is.

When boundaries are delineated, collective activation becomes information rather than identity.

Participation does not require fusion.

The invisible crowd is still a crowd.

Perceptual coherence is still available within it.

Boundaries allow you to remain yourself while the environment shifts.

The same principles that apply in physical crowds apply in digital ones.

The question is not whether you participate, but how clearly your boundary is organized while you do.

A Note on Online Harassment

Digital activation is not always neutral.

There are moments when the load on boundaries does not arise from amplification, but from deliberate targeting. Harassment, shaming, coordinated hostility, and sustained attack place a different strain on regulation.

In these situations, your system is not responding to synchrony. It is responding to threat.

Repeated negative exposure may produce:

> hypervigilance
> contraction of perceptual space
> intrusive thought cycles
> emotional spillover
> difficulty disengaging

This is not oversensitivity. It is a physiological response to sustained pressure.

Boundary clarity in these contexts may require:

> disengagement
> blocking or filtering
> reducing exposure
> reinforcing containment
> seeking appropriate support

Regulation does not mean enduring harm. Participation in digital environments is optional. Safety is not.

Boundaries are not only perceptual tools. They are protective limits.

A Note on When Activation Persists

Sometimes activation does not resolve when exposure ends.

If contraction, dread, or destabilization continue beyond the immediate context, the appropriate response may not be greater openness, but reduced exposure and additional support.

Regulation is not meant to be solitary.

Prolonged exposure to adversarial or high-load environments can tax the regulatory system. Over time, this may resemble patterns associated with anxiety, irritability, withdrawal, or low mood.

This does not mean digital environments "cause" distress in isolation. Human emotional states are multifactorial. It does mean that repeated boundary load without recovery can strain regulation.

If symptoms persist, intensify, or interfere with daily functioning, professional support may be appropriate.

Clear boundaries support not only perception, but psychological stability.

Pause. Check resonance.

EXPLORATION 11.6: The invisible Crowd Check
The Scroll Reset

Objective

To notice how your boundary responds to repeated or emotionally charged digital exposure, and to practice remaining oriented while engaging.

Setup

Choose a piece of digital content (news, commentary, social media, video, or discussion) that evokes a noticeable emotional tone. This exploration works best with real-time exposure rather than memory.

Sit upright with both of your feet grounded.

Steps

1. Engage briefly:
   → Scroll, read, or watch for 1–2 minutes.
   → Do not analyze the content.
   → Simply notice your internal state.
   → Allow whatever activation arises to take shape without evaluation.
2. Pause without closing. Keep the content visible but shift your attention to your body. Notice:
   → breath rhythm
   → chest or belly sensation
   → jaw or shoulder tension
   → emotional tone (heavy, sharp, warm, contracted, expansive)
   → urgency level
   → pull to continue (desire to scroll, click, or respond)
3. Withdraw your attention:
   → Set the device down or turn the screen away.
   → Let your eyes rest on something neutral in the room.
   → Take 3 slow, even breaths.
4. Reorient physically:
   → Feel your feet.
   → Adjust your posture.
   → Place your attention along the perimeter of your body until it feels distinct and contained.

5. Compare states. Notice:
   - → What changed when your attention withdrew?
   - → Did your emotional tone soften or persist?
   - → Did urgency decrease?
   - → Did clarity increase?
   - → Did the content feel different once your boundary was stabilized?
6. Optional return:
   - → Re-engage the same content for 30 seconds.
   - → Notice whether activation rises again.
7. Close deliberately:
   - → End the session intentionally rather than drifting.
   - → Set the device out of reach.
   - → Let your attention return fully to the room.
   - → Take 1 steady breath and allow your boundary to settle.

What to Watch For

> your breath shortening during exposure
> a forward lean or narrowing of your focus
> your emotional tone intensifying before evaluation
> identity language appearing internally
> relief or resistance when withdrawing attention

Reflection

↺ Did activation precede understanding?
↺ Did repetition increase certainty or intensity?
↺ Did stepping away restore clarity or create discomfort?
↺ Was the content stable under perceptual coherence, or did its force depend on immersion?

Why This Happens

Digital intensity organizes attention through repetition and emotional salience. When exposure is continuous, boundaries tend to thin gradually rather than abruptly. Activation becomes normalized.

By pausing without closing the content, you interrupt automatic synchronization while the stimulus remains present. By withdrawing your attention, you allow your perceptual coherence to reassert itself and observe what persists under regulation.

Signal that weakens under stabilization was likely amplified arousal rather than grounded perception.

This exploration is not about avoiding engagement.

It is about restoring regulatory choice.

Pause. Check resonance.

EXPLORATION 11.7: The Boundary Repair
Rebuilding Clarity After Collapse

Note

Sometimes signals are missed. Sometimes capacity changes. This exploration
is for those moments.

Objective

To restore a sense of containment when your boundary feels thin, diffuse, or
absent.

Setup

Sit or stand comfortably. Let your feet make contact with the ground.

Steps

1. Begin with slow, even breathing (for example, 5 seconds in, 5 seconds out).
2. Place your attention on a smooth, comfortable perimeter around your body,
   close enough to feel contained, wide enough to breathe easily.
3. On the exhale, allow that perimeter to firm and stabilize.
4. On the inhale, let it soften slightly without losing its shape.
5. Continue for several breaths, keeping your attention lightly on the perimeter
   and allowing clarity to return gradually.

What to Watch For

> a return of orientation
> overwhelm easing
> thoughts becoming quieter or more ordered
> a renewed sense of confidence or self-trust

Reflection

↺ What shifted when your system was no longer absorbing more than it could
hold?
↺ Did containment feel relieving rather than restrictive?

Why This Happens

When a boundary collapses (through fatigue, overwhelm, or prolonged openness), your system loses a clear sense of containment.

This can show up as:

> emotional spillover
> cognitive noise
> difficulty distinguishing self from environment

Slow, even breathing stabilizes autonomic tone.

Placing your attention on a defined space around you helps to restore spatial orientation.

Together, these cues signal safety to your nervous system, allowing your organismic intelligence to reorganize without force. Boundary repair is not an act of defense. It is a return to baseline organization: functional, and sufficient for clear participation.

Notes.

INTEGRATION PRACTICE 11
The Boundary Check-In

Several times a day, pause briefly and ask:

1. Where is my boundary right now? Wide, neutral, or close?
2. Has it thinned or collapsed? If so, restore it with 1 steady breath.
3. Is it too open for this environment? Gently contract.
4. Is it too tight for this task or relationship? Soften and widen.
5. Can I adjust before entering a space or conversation?

This is perceptual leadership: the capacity to regulate orientation before confusion or overwhelm arise.

<table>
<tr><td>Observations.

</td></tr>
</table>

Complicating factors can alter internal processes long before they are consciously recognized.

— Adapted from Ingo Swann, *Encountering Disorder and Complicating Factors Without Recognizing Them As Such*

Notes.

Closing Thought

Your boundary is not an abstraction. It is embodied and responsive.

Your perceptual space is not fixed. It adapts to context, intensity, repetition, and capacity.

Intensity may arise in a room full of people. It may also arise through a screen.

Your perceptual awareness system responds to signaling, whether it comes from physical proximity or amplified attention.

As you attune to your boundary, you begin to:

> stop absorbing what isn't yours
> remain oriented in high-energy environments
> engage digital intensity without being captured by it
> move through crowds without depletion
> step away from repetition without disorientation
> connect without merging
> register emotion without being overtaken

This is not withdrawal. It is participation with clarity.

> It is not defense.
> It is differentiation.

And differentiation is agency.

CODA

WHEN PERCEPTION BECOMES TRUSTWORTHY

Opening Invitation

You did not move through this book by trying to become extraordinary.

You moved through it by finding your footing within what you already perceive.

Along the way, you experienced that:

> perceptual coherence is a real state, not a metaphor
> emotion is texture, temperature, and movement, not just narrative
> boundaries are living membranes that expand, contract, and repair
> your body has a somatic yes and no that often speaks before thought
> intensity and charisma amplify what you perceive, and boundary clarity determines whether that amplification nourishes or overwhelms
> small, deliberate shifts in breath, posture, and attention change how everything feels

You discovered something essential:

> The exchange between awareness and perception does not become trustworthy because you see more.
> It becomes trustworthy because your system can hold what it becomes aware of.

Nothing in this book asked you to push further out. It asked you to stand more steadily where you already are.

What You Have Already Reclaimed

Across these chapters, you have:

1. **Organized your system.**
   You mapped how breath, posture, attention, and emotional tone can come into phase so your perceptual-awareness interchange feels less effortful.

2. **Met emotion as information.**
   You explored emotional "frequencies" as texture (heavy or light, sharp or soft, expansive, or contracted) so feeling became data rather than verdict.

3. **Tracked emotional influence.**
   You began to notice how your current tone quietly shapes what you register, how you interpret, and how you relate.

4. **Felt boundaries as real.**
   You experienced your perimeter as a sensing edge: adaptive, responsive, and adjustable, capable of maintaining clarity even in high-intensity environments.

5. **Recovered somatic consent.**
   You noticed how your body signals yes and no before language appears, and how that signal can coexist with reflection and choice.

6. **Recognized amplification.**
   You observed that not all boundary challenges arise from threat, how highly energized people, crowds, and collective excitement can amplify signaling and synchronize attention and emotion, placing unusual load on perceptual boundaries.

7. **Noticed collective signaling in digital space.**
   You saw that repetition, visibility, and collective reaction in digital environments can synchronize emotional tone across large networks, organizing attention and perception much like physical crowds.

8. **Practiced repair instead of collapse.**
   You discovered that when coherence frays, emotional tone spikes, or boundaries thin, you can reset rather than shut down or push through.

9. **None of this is a new ability.**
   It is awareness... attuning to a system that has always been working within you.

Why Stability Alone Is Not Enough

Stability changes everything. It also reveals more. As your system became more coherent and better boundaried, you may have noticed:

> subtler impressions arriving more often
> symbolic or layered material appearing at the edges of your awareness
> a sense of momentum or direction before events unfold
> old distortions (fear, bias, wishful thinking) trying to hijack meaning
> your intellect rushing in to explain what your body has just recorded
> intensity spreading rapidly in groups or around highly energized people
> emotional tone amplifying quickly through repetition or shared attention

Stability makes these experiences workable. But clarity requires something further:

> recognizing how information entered awareness
> distinguishing signal from projection
> distinguishing amplification from accuracy
> noticing when repetition strengthens conviction
> interpreting without collapsing into story
> staying oriented when multiple layers are active at once

That is the territory of the next book.

The Pivot into Book Three

Book Two asked:

How do I stabilize my system so what I perceive can be trusted?

Book Three begins to ask:

What, exactly, am I perceiving, and through which pathways?

You will explore:

1. **Multiple pathways of perception.**
   How literal sensing, felt inference, and symbolic perception each carry information differently.

2. **Symbolic cognition.**
   How images, metaphors, and patterns arise when linear perception cannot carry the full load, and how to work with them without inflation or fear.

3. **Distortion and noise.**
   How bias, emotional charge, desire, fatigue, and story twist perception, and how to recognize these patterns before believing them.

4. **Timeline sensitivity.**
   How your system registers momentum and direction (what is beginning, gathering, or fading) without pretending to predict the future.

5. **Clean interpretation.**
   How meaning forms from the bottom up: body → tone → relational context → symbol → direction, rather than jumping straight to conclusion.

If Book One was about noticing, and Book Two about holding,

Book Three explores the landscape of meaning: how knowing takes shape from perception.

Closing Thought

You have already proven that:

> your body can function as a stable sensing instrument
> your emotions can inform without overrunning you
> your boundaries can protect without isolating you
> your system can return to coherence, again and again

You no longer have to choose between sensitivity and stability.

You know how to have both.

What comes next is not about becoming more special.

It is about becoming more accurate, about seeing how information actually moves through you, where it bends, and how to stay clear as it deepens.

You now have:

> a coherent base
> emotional literacy
> living boundaries

Book Three begins from there (with the architecture of perception itself) so you can move into more complex layers of experience without losing your center, your clarity, or yourself.

APPENDIX

Quick Reset Practices

The brief resets below are not techniques to master or practices to perform regularly. They are simple ways of returning your system to a workable state when it drifts, intensifies, or becomes unclear.

You may use them as needed, or not at all.

Body Reset
(returning to physical presence)

> Exhale longer than you inhale.
> Relax your shoulders.
> Feel a connection to the ground through your feet or seat.
> Drop into the present moment.

Boundary Reset
(restoring perceptual containment)

> Inhale → gently gather your attention to your perimeter.
> Exhale → allow your boundary to close.
> Focus on a soft containment around the body.

Coherence Reset
(stabilizing rhythm and tone)

> Inhale for 5 seconds.
> Exhale for 5 seconds.
> Bring to mind something you appreciate.
> Let your attention smooth and stabilize.

Emotional Check-In
(staying oriented with feeling)

> Where is the sensation located?
> What is its texture?
> What is its direction (up / down / inward / outward)?
> Can it soften with one breath?

Perceptual Reorientation
(returning to balanced attention)

> Turn your attention inward.
> Soften your visual focus.
> Allow your awareness to include the room around you.

SELECTED SCIENTIFIC & PHILOSOPHICAL FOUNDATIONS

The following works have informed the biological, regulatory, relational, and phenomenological perspectives that shape this book.

They are not cited exhaustively, but represent foundational contributions in autonomic regulation, interoception, emotional construction, peripersonal space, boundary perception, social synchrony, and embodied cognition.

The explorations in this book draw upon established findings in heart–brain interaction, neurovisceral integration, autonomic regulation, emotional contagion, co-regulation, proxemics, and spatial boundary mapping.

They are phenomenological exercises (structured observations of lived experience) grounded in contemporary neuroscience and embodied cognition.

References

Argyle, M., & Cook, M. (1976). *Gaze and mutual gaze*. Cambridge University Press.

Barrett, L. F. (2017). *How emotions are made: The secret life of the brain*. Houghton Mifflin Harcourt.

Barrett, L. F., & Simmons, W. K. (2015). Interoceptive predictions in the brain. *Nature Reviews Neuroscience, 16*(7),

Blanke, O., & Arzy, S. (2005). The out-of-body experience: Disturbed self-processing at the temporo-parietal junction. *The Neuroscientist, 11*(1), 16–24.

Clark, A. (2016). *Surfing uncertainty: Prediction, action, and the embodied mind*. Oxford University Press.

Cléry, J., Guipponi, O., Wardak, C., & Ben Hamed, S. (2015). Neuronal bases of peripersonal and extrapersonal space processing. *Journal of Neuroscience,*

Craig, A. D. (2002). How do you feel? Interoception: The sense of the physiological condition of the body. *Nature Reviews Neuroscience, 3*(8), 655–666.

Critchley, H. D., & Garfinkel, S. N. (2017). Interoception and emotion. *Current Opinion in Psychology, 17,* 7–14.

Damasio, A. (1999). *The feeling of what happens: Body and emotion in the making of consciousness*. Harcourt Brace.

Damasio, A. (2010). *Self comes to mind: Constructing the conscious brain*. Pantheon Books.

Feldman, R. (2012). Parent–infant synchrony: A biobehavioral model of mutual influences in the formation of affiliative bonds. *Monographs of the Society for Research in Child Development, 77*(2), 42–51.

Friston, K. (2010). The free-energy principle: A unified brain theory? *Nature Reviews Neuroscience, 11*(2), 127–138.

Gallagher, S. (2005). *How the body shapes the mind*. Oxford University Press.

Graziano, M. S. A. (2010). The intelligent movement machine: An evolutionary perspective on the neural basis of emotional experience. *Consciousness and Cognition, 19*(1), 98–110.

Graziano, M. S. A., & Cooke, D. F. (2006). Parieto-frontal interactions, personal space, and defensive behavior. *Neuropsychologia, 44*(13), 2621–2635.

Hall, E. T. (1966). *The hidden dimension*. Doubleday.

Hatfield, E., Cacioppo, J. T., & Rapson, R. L. (1993). Emotional contagion. *Current Directions in Psychological Science, 2*(3), 96–100.

Hohwy, J. (2013). *The predictive mind.* Oxford University Press.

Kahneman, D. (2011). *Thinking, fast and slow.* Farrar, Straus and Giroux.

Khalsa, S. S., Adolphs, R., Cameron, O. G., Critchley, H. D., Davenport, P. W., Feinstein, J. S., et al. (2018). Interoception and mental health: A roadmap. Biological Psychiatry: Cognitive Neuroscience and Neuroimaging, 3(6), 501–513.

Konvalinka, I., & Roepstorff, A. (2012). The two-brain approach: Studying interaction in social neuroscience. *Frontiers in Human Neuroscience, 6,* 215.

Levenson, R. W., & Gottman, J. M. (1983). Marital interaction: Physiological linkage and affective exchange. *Journal of Personality and Social Psychology, 45*(3), 587–597.

McCraty, R., & Shaffer, F. (2015). Heart rate variability: New perspectives on physiological mechanisms and health risk. *Global Advances in Health and Medicine, 4*(1), 46–61.

Merleau-Ponty, M. (2012). *Phenomenology of perception* (D. A. Landes, Trans.). Routledge. (Original work published 1945)

Noble, D. J., & Hochman, S. (2019). Pulmonary afferent activity during slow breathing and relaxation. *Frontiers in Physiology, 10,* 1176.

Palumbo, R. V., et al. (2017). Interpersonal autonomic physiology: A systematic review. *Personality and Social Psychology Review, 21*(2), 99–141.

Panksepp, J. (1998). *Affective neuroscience: The foundations of human and animal emotions.* Oxford University Press.

Porges, S. W. (2009). The polyvagal theory: New insights into adaptive reactions of the autonomic nervous system. *Cleveland Clinic Journal of Medicine, 76*(Suppl 2), S86–S90.

Porges, S. W. (2011). *The polyvagal theory: Neurophysiological foundations of emotions, attachment, communication, and self-regulation.* W. W. Norton.

Raichle, M. E., MacLeod, A. M., Snyder, A. Z., Powers, W. J., Gusnard, D. A., & Shulman, G. L. (2001). A default mode of brain function. *Proceedings of the National Academy of Sciences, 98*(2), 676–682.

Rao, R. P. N., & Ballard, D. H. (1999). Predictive coding in the visual cortex: A functional interpretation of some extra-classical receptive-field effects. *Nature Neuroscience, 2*(1), 79–87.

Rizzolatti, G., & Sinigaglia, C. (2008). *Mirrors in the brain: How our minds share actions and emotions*. Oxford University Press.

Senju, A., & Johnson, M. H. (2009). The eye contact effect. *Trends in Cognitive Sciences, 13*(3), 127–134.

Seth, A. (2021). *Being you: A new science of consciousness*. Dutton.

Seth, A. K., & Friston, K. J. (2016). Active interoceptive inference and the emotional brain. *Philosophical Transactions of the Royal Society B: Biological Sciences, 371*(1708), 20160007.

Shaffer, F., & Ginsberg, J. P. (2017). An overview of heart rate variability metrics and norms. *Frontiers in Public Health, 5*, 258.

Swann, I. (1997, October 15). *Encountering disorder and complicating factors without recognizing them as such*. Biomind Superpowers.

Swann, I. (1997, December 12). *Contaminants and "noise"*. Biomind Superpowers.

Swann, I. (1998, March 1). *Sentiency and sensitivity*. Biomind Superpowers.

Swann, I. (1999, October 2). *Awareness and perception vs status of individual "realities"*. Biomind Superpowers.

Swann, I. (2002a, August 8). *Sentiency and sensitivity, the topic of the human species guild revisited six years later*. Biomind Superpowers.

Swann, I. (2002b). *Secrets of power, Volume II: The vitalizing of individual powers*. Ingo Swann Books.

Swann, I. (2018). *Psychic literacy: & the coming psychic renaissance*. Swann-Ryder Productions, LLC.

Teneggi, C., Canzoneri, E., di Pellegrino, G., & Serino, A. (2013). Social modulation of peripersonal space boundaries. *Current Biology, 23*(5), 406–411.

Thayer, J. F., Åhs, F., Fredrikson, M., Sollers, J. J., III, & Wager, T. D. (2012). A meta-analysis of heart rate variability and neuroimaging studies: Implications for heart rate variability as a marker of stress and health. *Neuroscience & Biobehavioral Reviews, 36*(2), 747–756.

Thayer, J. F., & Lane, R. D. (2000). A model of neurovisceral integration in emotion regulation. *Journal of Affective Disorders, 61*(3), 201–216.

Thompson, E. (2007). *Mind in life: Biology, phenomenology, and the sciences of mind*. Harvard University Press.

Tsakiris, M., & Critchley, H. D. (2016). Interoception beyond homeostasis: Affect, cognition, and mental health. *Philosophical Transactions of the Royal Society B: Biological Sciences, 371*(1708), 20160002.

Varela, F. J., Thompson, E., & Rosch, E. (1991). *The embodied mind: Cognitive science and human experience.* MIT Press.

THE SERIES
You Are More Than You Think

Book One
What's Already There

Book Two
Where You Sit

Book Three
The Shape of Knowing

Book Four
Above the Noise

Book Five
The Gravity of Reality

Chapter numbers continue across volumes to reflect that the series unfolds as one integrated structure rather than as separate works. Each book stands on its own, but the numbering maintains the progression for readers who move across the entire sequence.

Elly Flippen is the niece of Ingo Swann and the editor of **Why Do We Feel There Is More to Us Than We, or Anyone, Knows About?**, as well as the author of **Conjunction.World**.

Her work is shaped by years of engagement with questions of perception, awareness, and the lived experience of human intelligence beyond habit and assumption.

She invites readers to rely on their own sensing and discernment, recognizing perception not as something to acquire, but as something already active and waiting to be understood.

To learn more about Ingo Swann and his work, visit **www.ingoswann.com**.